# #BOY MOM

How today's moms can embrace and enjoy
the adventure of raising sons

Kimberly C. Miller

# CONTENTS

# INTRODUCTION

The door opened with a crash and they flung themselves through the opening. Stumbling into the kitchen, they raced around the table, making as much noise as possible for people their size. In a fury of commotion, they tumbled onto the living room rug, tangled in what appeared to be half bear hug, half wrestling match.

"Boys!" I exclaimed. "You know you're not supposed to play like that in the house. Head outside!"

The older one hopped up and raced for the door. "Beat you to the swing set!" He yelled behind him at his younger brother, who was close on his heels. They sped out the door, slamming it behind them as they went.

Suddenly, the room was quiet again.

If you're a mom of boys, you know this scene can happen with perplexing frequency. Moments like the one I just described have often left me either scratching my head in wonder, or sighing with frustration.

Boys tend to be loud. They tend to have unlimited amounts of energy. They can be destructive, either accidentally or, at times, on purpose. Often, their interests include things that are dangerous, harmful, or just plain disgusting.

Have you ever looked at your son and wondered what on earth was going on inside his head? Have you ever wished you had some insight into how to manage and direct all the natural energy boys have? Maybe you've thought to yourself, "Is this interest my son is pursuing even normal?"

Let's face it, raising boys can be a challenge for us moms. We don't always know what makes them tick. We can't understand where their boundless energy comes from. We wonder why in the world every stick (or grilled cheese sandwich, for that matter) becomes a potential weapon.

We also wonder if we're doing something wrong. Why does our little guy have such a hard time sitting still when our friend's daughter can sit quietly and occupy herself for hours? Why does our son's brand new pair of jeans only last a month before the knees wear out? Why do their faces and hands seem to be constantly dirty, no matter how often throughout the day we take them to the sink to wash them?

As a mother of eight living children, five of whom are sons, I've experienced pretty much everything a mom of boys can—all the joys, and all the challenges, all the moments that make you want to scratch your head in bewilderment, and all the times when your heart swells with pride and overflows with love for this man-in-the-making who calls you "mommy." I've seen it all, and then some.

Over the years, I've had other mothers of boys ask me for advice on how to handle certain behaviors or tendencies. Mostly the questions revolve around how to keep them busy and out of trouble. Often moms' concerns are connected with their sons' education and schooling experience. It's easy to get frustrated or confused by the things our boys do sometimes. Standard advice in today's culture is to just change the boys. But is that the best and most effective approach? And is it even fair to these wonderful, amazing human beings who represent half the world's population?

For decades, our approach to raising boys is to smash them into a mold that was never designed for anything even remotely boy-shaped. Our sons have been the proverbial round shaped pegs we've tried to jam into the square-shaped hole of societal standards. We've told boys there is something inherently wrong with them—that they are too much, or not enough.

It's time to stop telling boys they are flawed for being who they are. It's time to start embracing boys in all their dirty, rambunctious glory. It's time to stop saying that God somehow made a mistake when He made our sons. God has a wonderful purpose for the way He designed boys, and we need to learn to appreciate and celebrate the wonders of that design.

In your hands you hold the sum of all the wisdom I've gleaned from decades spent raising a houseful of sons. Any mom of boys will tell you it's not an easy feat. I've made plenty of mistakes; my sons can attest to that fact. I have, however, learned a thing or two about how boys tick and how to love and embrace what makes them who they are.

Where can we go for answers to the challenges we face as moms of sons? Are there even answers available, or are we on our own in figuring things out? I have good news—there are answers. There is a treasure trove of knowledge to unlock and dive into when learning how to be a great mom of boys. So much wisdom and understanding is available to assist us in living with, loving and raising these incredible creatures.

In these pages, I'd like to share with you some of the knowledge and experience I have learned over my career as a mom of five normal, active boys. I hope you will find what I have learned to be helpful and encouraging as you walk this amazing path of being a #boymom.

# CHAPTER ONE

When I was expecting my first child, people asked me many times, like they do most new parents, if I wanted a girl or boy. To be honest, it really didn't matter either way to me. I was, however, absolutely convinced for some reason that I was having a girl. Maybe it was because I felt I was better equipped to raise a girl. The thought of having a boy was overwhelming to me. Actually, the thought of being a mother in general was overwhelming. I've always been the type of person who likes to get my feet wet before jumping into a new experience. Anyone who has had children knows there is no easing your way in. You're either all in or not at all. So, my reasoning, though not even really fully developed, was extremely flawed. However, that was where my head was as I waited for my firstborn's arrival.

On the day my first child was born, I had the delightful experience of being surprised by being blessed with a tiny, beautiful baby boy. He arrived 5 days past his due date and my labor was medically induced because my amniotic fluid levels were very low. Labor only lasted 5 hours, and I made it through without medication—a feat I was absolutely determined to achieve. We spent two days in the hospital, then we were sent home.

To say my husband's and my first days home with our first child were a trial by fire would be an understatement. For the first 18 hours of being home, our new little bundle of joy cried almost non-stop. Learning to nurse him was a struggle; we both had no idea what we were doing. But just like with the unmedicated birth, I was determined to make this thing work. Exhaustion and postpartum depression set in quickly. I was convinced there was something seriously wrong with me. Through many years of experience since then, I know now it wasn't me, and it wasn't the baby for that matter. He was just an especially high needs child. As he has grown, and I have seen the man he has become and the talents and preferences he has developed, I realize now some of the mistakes I made and some of the reasons he was the way he was as a small child. But at the time, I just thought I was a failure as a new mom.

Fast forward 4 years to when my second child was born. We found out ahead of time whether this baby was a girl or boy. We were excited to find that our son would have a little brother. I did wonder, however, if God was secretly chuckling at the thought of making me the mom of two boys, especially when most of my friends had sweet, quiet, compliant little girls, while I was chasing around a precocious, energetic little boy who couldn't sit still for more that three seconds and didn't want to sleep for more than 7 hours in any given 24 hour stretch.

The period of time after my second son's birth was completely different than after my first son was born. From the beginning, my second got himself onto a regular sleep schedule. He learned to nurse like a champ from the beginning. He only cried when he was hungry or needed his diaper changed. His moods and preferences were steady and reliable. (He is still this way to this day.) Having such dramatically different experiences with my first two children made me realize that, although I took the same type of approach to mothering both of them, they were two completely different people. They each had individual preferences, tendencies, and abilities.

Each child is uniquely their own person, created by God for a specific purpose. This truth, though one of my biggest challenges as a young mother, is one of my greatest delights now that I have years of experience and knowledge under my belt. Seeing each of my children develop and grow as people, with their unique personalities and gifts to offer to the world, has been an amazing experience.

Why am I sharing all of this with you here? Because I want to assure you that even though you may feel like somehow you are failing because your child is more challenging to raise, you are not. We underestimate the wonder and the blessing of raising out-of-the-box children for God's glory. Focusing on the gifts our children bring to the world will help us look at them with compassion and understanding and be patient with the ways in which they might be different.

For the record, my third child was a girl, and the experience of her early years was so completely different from that of my first two sons, that it solidified my own realization that I wasn't doing anything majorly wrong with my kids—they were all just very different and very wonderful in their own unique ways. My daughter was the epitome of the quiet, sweet little girl. Now, I realize that not all girls are like that, any more than all boys are interested in sports or video games. Now that she is older, my daughter is actually very outdoorsy and can be quite tough when she needs to be. It's how she looks at the world, and responds to it, that makes up the difference between her (and her sisters) and her brothers.

Boys are, by nature, different from girls. That truth should be obvious, but in today's culture, I'm afraid the waters have been muddied a bit in this area. However, simple observation on the playground will show that boy deal with varying situations differently than girls do. Talking with them for more than five minutes can reveal how differently they think about the world around them. Examining their interests and tendencies can, for the most part, show how vastly different they can be. That's not to say that boys can't like baby dolls or girls don't play with matchbox cars—both things have happened in my house. However, their basic makeup and the way they interact with life is undeniably in contrast with one another.

**Anatomy**

Let's take something as basic as anatomy. Obviously, we all know that male and female bodies differ from one another. There is a contrast between the way a girl's body is put together and the way a boy's is. Boys are made one way with one purpose, girls are made another way with another. As they grow into men and women, their bodies change and develop in very different ways. Their hormones develop differently. All of this really goes without saying, however its is important to point out as it illustrates a further truth I would like to express.

If we can look at our children and see their physical differences and accept them as natural and normal, shouldn't we be able to say the same about their behavioral differences, their differing preferences and interests, and their different tendencies and capabilities? Shouldn't we be able to respect the fact that God made boys differently than girls for a very specific purpose and even celebrate and praise those differences?

## Energy

As a young mother of small boys, I was surrounded by friends who had only girls. So many of my closest friends at the time were first time moms of daughters, and it made me feel like there was something drastically wrong with my parenting abilities. I could not figure out why my little boys were always moving, always getting into things, always needing a project to keep them busy, when my friends girls would sit and play with the same toy for 45 minutes without making a peep.

It took me a long time to realize that it was okay for my boys to be busy and to always be moving around. It didn't mean there was something wrong with them. There wasn't anything about who they were that needed to change. Just because they were different from the little girls around them didn't mean that was a negative thing. It was actually good that they were different. After all, they were not girls, so why should they behave just like them?

Boys have lots of energy. That fact is well established and easily observable. Boys need to be doing things. This higher energy level is a gift from God. He has equipped them to do the work in life He wants them to do.

It is unfair to expect boys to sit still and quiet for long periods of time. It is unfair to expect children in general to do so—they are not small adults. However, it is even more so for boys. They have an innate need to conquer something. Way back in the Garden of Eden, God commanded Adam to take dominion over the earth, to work at tilling the soil and managing the animals. From the start, men have had the responsibility of work, and work requires energy.

In young boys, this large amount of energy can and should be directed and channelled. It can be used in productive ways. I talk more about practical ways to do that in a later chapter. For now, just remember that if your boy is active, energetic, and constantly moving, congratulations! You have a perfectly normal, healthy son!

**Brain Function**

Studies show that the male and female brain function differently from one another. Men think differently than women do.[1] This starts early in life. Even young boys show obvious male traits in their thinking patterns and brain function.

Differences in brain function will affect how boys and girls process any given situation. It affects how they perform in school. These differences affect their interests and even how they approach a new experience. Language processing and development is also an often overlooked area where these differences in brain function are especially evident in boys and girls.

Never underestimate the power of brain function in affecting every area of the lives of our sons.

**Interests and enjoyment**

Boys, when given the choice, often choose leisure activities that differ from what a girl might choose. Sports, video games, and building projects are all examples of ways in which boys enjoy spending their times. An important thing to notice is that these activities involve conquering some obstacle. Observe your son sometime when he in engaged in an activity he especially enjoys and notice how the object of the activity relates to his overcoming some challenge. The innate, God given need boys have to take dominion is often expressed in their playtime. It is the early, undeveloped evidence of a call to rise up and take charge of their own lives and the things in their lives they must be responsible for. Encourage it—help them think big, even when they themselves are still little. It will set up patterns in their thinking that will help them accomplish big things in their lives when they are grown.

Many times, boys find things humorous that most moms would find disgusting or perplexing. Gross out humor, goofiness, and just plain silliness are all hallmarks of boyish humor. Even my older boys and their dad often laugh at things I find completely unfunny! This tendency in differences in humor goes back to brain function and reasoning. Though I will never understand it, I have come to accept it as a normal part of raising boys. My advice to you is to do the same; don't try to figure it out, just embrace it as part of being the mother of a son.

Why are boys entertained by things like mud, trucks, and swords? Boys gravitate toward mud like they are magnetized by it. How do even small boys (often before they can even talk) instinctively know how to make the sound of a motor? Isn't it amazing how they do that? Boys see the world differently, and so are entertained by different types of things.

**Celebrate the Uniqueness**

The many ways in which boys are so dramatically different from girls is a wonderful gift to the world around them. God uniquely created them to fulfill a special role in this world. These differences are powerful and have a great impact. We can embrace who God made them to be, knowing it was with a specific reason in mind. We are not like our sons. They are not like the girls around them. That is a beautiful and important truth to remember.

In the next chapter, we will take a more in-depth look at how boys develop throughout their childhood. There are so many areas in which boys display their boyishness through their development. Let's examine how this plays out and how it affects our role as their moms.

# CHAPTER TWO

## Development

Boys, like girls, go through different stages of development throughout their growing-up years. Though each child's growth and development is unique to them, there are certain established patterns that most children follow as they journey through their childhood and into adulthood. It is well known by parents, psychologists, and medical professionals that boys develop in similar ways as girls, but often on differing time tables and to varying degrees.[2]

Growing up is never an easy process for anyone. The emotional, physical, and mental changes that take place in a human being as he or she moves into adulthood can often be challenging and confusing. Navigating childhood can be tough. Boys is our present society have it even tougher in many cases. The mere fact of their maleness is one strike against them, I'm afraid. They're naturally noisy, dirty, aggressive, energetic, and take any challenge head on with great gusto. These traits are not ones considered acceptable in our culture. Moms often feel the pressure somehow to work these traits out of their sons so they will be more socially acceptable. Prescription drugs, "behavioral therapies," and other forms of "help" are often designed to extract out of boys the very things that make them who they are.

## Infancy

As infants, boys are often more active than girls. Baby boys move more, they wiggle and squirm more, and they don't spend nearly as much time in quiet observational mode as baby girls do. The higher activity level boys typically exhibit throughout childhood usually begins at birth.

Baby boys prefer to watch moving objects over stationary ones. They are drawn to motion. Recent studies have shown that baby boys develop the understanding of the laws of motion at a slightly earlier age than girls (about two months). For instance, boys figure out earlier that if a ball rolls under one side of the table, they should look for it on the other side. It usually takes girls longer to understand that concept.

Boys in infancy prefer to look at groups of faces rather than a single face, as opposed to girls, who like to focus on one particular face to interact with. Baby boys are generally more comfortable in crowds that baby girls are. And baby boys exhibit fewer signs of fearful reactions to new situations or loud noises. Even at an early age, boys are often what we would call fearless.

## Toddlerhood

No, it's not your imagination that your son instinctively learned to make the sound of a car motor, or that it varies in pitch depending on whether he's pushing a Tonka truck or a matchbox car. As mentioned before, baby boys naturally notice moving objects. Their attention gravitates toward movement. By the time they reach 18 months to 2 years, they have mastered an early understanding of how moving objects function. They have also noticed the sounds those objects make. The bigger the object, the more notice they take of it. Large, moving objects are like magnets for toddler boys.

Language development is typically later for boys than for girls. Girls usually begin to mimic sounds early in their development and begin talking at a slightly younger age than boys do. Boys are simply too busy moving and doing to pay much attention to the talking going on around them. Research shows it is possible that genetics or hormonal differences can also account for the differing ways in which boys' and girls' brains react to speech and speech development.[3] Girls also tend to be better at reading nonverbal forms of communication.

In terms of motor skills, boys usually develop gross motor skills faster (jumping, running, balancing) and girls tend to be earlier in fine motor skill development (holding a pencil, writing). This fact is extremely important to remember as boys reach school age. They simply cannot perform the physical act of writing with a pencil on paper for as long as girls can or with as much precision. Understanding this will help free a lot of boys from unreasonable expectations often placed on them in a school environment (and even sometimes in a homeschooling situation).[4]

Toddler boys tend to have more bumps and bruises as they grow through their early childhood days. This can often be attributed to the fact that they interact with their world in a more physical way. They have fewer fears. As a result, they naturally tend to take more risks when it comes to movement and trying new activities.

One day, when my second son (remember, he's the "quiet" one in my bunch of boys) was around 8 months old, I came out of the bathroom to discover him sitting on the high, wide windowsill above our living room couch. How he managed to climb up the back of the couch and onto the windowsill, I have no idea. But there he was, happily looking out the window while precariously perched on the narrow sill.

A friend of mine had three boys under the age of two (the second and third were twins) and she tells me she had to install hooks high up on the walls of her dining room to hang her chairs on because she could not keep her toddler aged twins from moving the chairs around and climbing on them in order to reach things too high for them to get to from the ground.

Little boys take risks. Big boys take even bigger risks. It is in a boy's nature to be a risk taker. It is literally part of their DNA.[5] (Here's a little piece of advice for my fellow moms who may be concerned or nervous upon discovering that fact about their boys: don't squelch it—channel it!)

Boys typically potty train later than girls. It's unclear from research whether this is due to physiologic differences or something in their social environment.[6] I just know it was true for my own boys. As a mother, potty training a little boy can be an interesting and sometimes intimidating experience, to say the least. My best advice is that, though you will most likely be the one doing the bulk of the actual potty training, getting dad involved can help the process go more smoothly. Something about a little guy seeing his daddy demonstrating what he needs to learn to do can help solidify his understanding and desire to perform this new skill for himself.

**Early school years**

As boys enter their early school years, new challenges begin to emerge for them in terms of development. A traditional school environment is designed to cater to the developmental stages typical of girls. As I mentioned earlier, boys usually develop fine motor skills much later than girls. Writing, therefore, can be physically difficult for a young boy to do. The ability to sit still for long periods of time is something young boys don't generally develop until much later. Focusing attention on one thing for an extended period of time can also be challenging for young boys who have not yet developed certain mental focussing abilities. Remember, boys' attention spans are wired for activity and movement.

Often, boys receive a diagnosis of ADHD when the "symptoms" they are exhibiting are normal behavioral tendencies for a boy in that stage of development. That is not to say that ADHD does not exist. However, it is often over diagnosed. A basic understanding of the mental and physical development of young boys could in some cases negate the need for a diagnosis like ADHD, especially if combined with a shift in the approach taken to their education. A typical traditional school setting is not conducive to the natural inclinations for learning exhibited in a boy of average development.

Let's give our boys a better chance at learning by looking for creative approaches to education that work with, not against, the way boys are designed to learn. I'll discuss this idea much more in depth in a later chapter.

## Middle school

The middle and junior high school years are challenging times of change for any child. Hormones are changing and surging, social expectations shift, there are new kinds of pressures from peers, school life takes on a different role. All this shifting and changing, inside and out, can cause a lot of confusion for both boys and girls. The difference comes in how boys and girls handle and respond to these changes and challenges.

While girls will often talk about their feelings, or develop deeper friendships, or perhaps even internalize a lot of what is happening to them, boys will usually act out how they are feeling in a much more external way. Anger, frustration, and aggression are some ways in which boys express the confusion and uncertainty they are feeling about the changes happening in and around them.

This time of transition can make any good parent of who

they formerly thought was a great kid begin wondering where they have gone wrong. Why is my son suddenly so angry all the time? Why does he seem so unsure of himself when in the past he has been so self confident? Why is he suddenly so aggressive toward others?

Rest assured, mom. Your middle school son is completely normal. Understand, that doesn't mean the aggressive or angry behavior should be tolerated. It absolutely must be addressed. Just like you taught your toddler son that taking a toy away from and hitting another child was wrong, he must also learn that taking his frustration out in forceful ways against others is not acceptable. Then he needs productive areas in his life in which to channel those aggressive feelings. We'll talk more about the specifics of how to do this in an upcoming chapter.

**Teen Years**

I am a firm believer that raising teenagers does not have to be a trial. There are challenges, I'll admit—many more than I expected before my own children reached their teen years. I had no idea of some of the areas I would be stretched as a mom when my children reached their teens. But raising teens has also been a full and enriching experience as well. Their preferences, talents, and individual personalities are developing rapidly and specifically. It can be such a joy to watch them unfold into who they are meant to become.

Like the middle school years, the teen years can be a volatile time. For boys, it is a time of trying to establish themselves as men, which brings with it a feeling on their part of needing to challenge authority. At this time in their development, boys want to feel respected as individuals. They want to be seen as men. They want to be seen for who they are meant to be, not just who they are right now. They need us as their moms to hope, to have faith in who God created them to be. More than anything, they want to be valued for their inherent potential as men.

Again, we see clear evidence in boys in their teens years as having a much higher level of aggressive tendencies than girls.[7] They continue to be much more action oriented. Pastimes that channel this natural, God given need for activity provide a healthy outlet. Boys at this age can benefit greatly from spending their time on pursuits that provide value to those around them and contribute their own personal sense of self worth. They will see themselves as valuable if they are making themselves useful and valuable to others. Give your teenage son something practical he can excel at and you will eliminate a lot of the behavioral problems common in today's teenage boys. Distract them from negative activities by giving them positive pursuits (work, sports, hobbies, academics, music) that require their energy and focus and give them a sense of bringing value into this world.

Teenage boys are, in reality, young men, and should be treated as such. They should be expected to behave as a young man would. Our society is so backwards in so many ways when it comes to raising boys. We have unreasonable and unrealistic expectations of our young sons. We want them to sit still, pay attention, and be quiet. When they don't meet those expectations (because they are not wired to), we label, medicate, and shame them. Then, as they grow older, we expect them to continue in the immature and irresponsible behavior of youth well into their late teens and twenties, long after they have physiologically become men. We are shortchanging our boys, and ourselves, by doing this. We need to shift our exceptions to match the natural development and abilities of our sons, so that we are giving them a leg up and encouraging them to fulfill their own potential as the amazing, life-changing men they are meant to be.

# CHAPTER THREE

Boys have lots of energy. It is safe to assume that boys of any age are energetic, active, and often very determined. It is in their makeup, inherent in the very fiber of their being. This boundless energy is a gift from God and one thing that make boys distinctly male.

I have to admit, as the mother of a houseful of sons, their energy can leave me exhausted at times. I can honestly say even on my best days, I have never in my entire life been able to sustain the level of activity my boys display on a continual basis. It's a wonder and a fascination to me to watch how much one small boy can do in the space of a few moments of expended effort. Whether it's building a block tower, playing a game of catch, or emptying an entire kitchen cabinet in a matter of minutes, boys do things with gusto!

My oldest son amazed me. As a young, first time mother, I did not know what to do with all that movement my son was constantly engaged in. It was unending motion, from sunrise to nap time, then again from then till bedtime. From one activity to the next, he was a busy, curious little person and at the end of the day, I was completely spent. I had to figure out a way of pacing myself, conserving my own stores of energy for the times when I really needed to be engaged with him. Very early in my mommy game, I discovered a little secret that has worked well in raising every one of my boys, even with their differing personalities and preferences. That secret isn't profound or difficult to come up with, but I find it's the number one piece of advice other moms of boys thank me for. The real secret to keeping up with your son's energetic approach to life? Give him something to do.

## Real-Life Problems to Solve

To keep boys busy and give them a sense of accomplishment and self worth, your job as the mom is to find projects to occupy his hands and his mind. Now, I'm not advocating that you schedule your son's time from dawn till dark. They need unstructured time to play and explore. But you can direct their attention toward activities that are productive and helpful rather than disruptive and destructive.

Giving a young boy direction for all that energy will help keep him out of trouble and keep you sane.

That doesn't mean you have to schedule or plan out every minute of his day. Children need free, unstructured time to play and explore the world and learn at their own pace. However, throughout the day, once in a while it can be helpful for both of you for you to have a suggestion for an activity that can direct some of that movement and noise into a useful project.

**Get him outside**

Boys need fresh air, space to run, and room to be loud. Their bodies need the physical outlet that time spent outside provides. Boys were not made to spend the major part of their days cooped up inside, doing quiet, calm activities. They do not have the physical capability to sustain that kind of control for any real length of time, especially when they are young. They are meant to be exploring, conquering, and doing. Let them have plenty of time outside, watching bugs, digging in dirt, climbing trees, walking on trails, playing sports, working on projects like mechanics or woodworking.

Any boy will respond to a challenge. Test him to see how fast he can run. Ask him to show you how many times he can catch the ball in a row. Show him how to build a whole town full of roads in the sand. He'll rise to the challenge and he will also love the physical impression he is making on the world around him. It will give him a sense of satisfaction to know that he has mastered something, no matter how small or useless the task may seem to us.

These kinds of outdoor activities contribute to brain development as well as helping the body to develop in a strong and healthy way. Girls need fresh air, too. However, the importance of getting outside to the life of a young boy cannot be overemphasized. It is essential to their wellbeing to spend time in the great outdoors.

So, what if you live in a city or a more suburban area where there are fewer opportunities for boys to spend large amounts of time outside? It may be more difficult to fit this outdoor time into your son's life, but it is not impossible. Make it a priority to seek out places and means for him to have that time. Take him on an afternoon walk to the park or playground. Get bicycles and ride to wherever you need to go throughout the day (if he is old enough to ride on his own). Be creative—ideas for how to provide outdoor activities will present themselves. Organized sports are available in almost every community—that can be a great way to help your active boy use up some of that energy in a positive way.

There will be times throughout the day when your son will be especially active and circumstances will not allow him to run it off in the backyard or at the park. Those are the times when you will need to find something to keep his hands busy (puzzles or coloring for younger ones, model building, making music, or drawing or some other activity for older ones).

**Let him be active**

It is essential to remember that boys have a naturally higher activity level than girls. Their voices are generally louder. They often make more noise. This is all completely normal. As moms, we sometimes think we need to quiet or calm ours sons down. A lot of our frustrations as moms of boys are tied to their activeness and noisiness. If we could learn to embrace those traits as some of what makes our sons who they are, we would do ourselves and our sons a huge favor.

We need to stop expecting our boys to be calm and quiet all the time—it's just not going to happen. They need to make noise. They need to be active. Their voices are the volume they are. That's not to say we shouldn't teach our boys how to have self-control when it is necessary. But we need to balance that with plenty of time to let out their naturally loud selves. They are not flawed because they are active and noisy. It is who they are. Let's learn to love and enjoy these amazing qualities in our sons. Those are the qualities that will contribute to making them into the world-changers they are meant to be.

Stifling our sons energy could have the effect of stifling their potential. They need to make a mark on the world. Let them do it!

I don't know about you, but I don't want to be the one who stands in the way of any of my sons reaching their full potential. I want to encourage them to take on big challenges in life. I want them to know that I will support them in expressing their God-given talents and abilities in amazing and really big ways. They need to know that their mom believes in them and that who they are as people is valuable and worthy. They can do big things with the energy bound up in them. We must teach them to let it out in productive ways. That's when they will be able to make a real difference in this world.

When you look at your son, do you see a dirty, loud, trouble making little boy, or do you see the ground-breaking, world-changing man he could become? Start training yourself to see that man, and you will be inspired in many ways in how to encourage him toward that end.

**Accept him for who he is**

Knowing that boys are naturally active, we can now accept that they will cause some degree of chaos and destruction. They are powerhouses of pent up potential waiting to be unleashed. Of course they will have an effect on their surroundings. It is natural to expect them to make an impact.

Some boys will be more destructive than others. Each one of my boys has caused their own level of catastrophe. It goes back to that bundled up energy and the fact that in their immaturity, boys don't yet know how to handle it or what to do with all of it. Be patient, mom. Remember what is most important. Doesn't your son mean more to you than that glass of spilled milk or broken picture frame? Take care to never make him feel as if you value the picture frame more than him. Be careful what message you are sending with your reactions to your son's behavior.

In saying all this, I am not advocating letting your son run wild and never reigning him in or teaching him self-control. It is essential that boys learn how to control themselves in any situation in which its is necessary. I am saying, however, that too many unrealistic expectations are put on our boys to act and behave in ways that are very difficult for them to achieve at certain points in their development.

Don't expect your son to sit quietly and unmoving for half

an hour when he is 3 years old. He can't physically do it. He will most likely wiggle and squirm a bit, and that's okay. Now, by the time he is 13 years old, he will have acquired the developmental ability to achieve this. Make sure your behavioral expectations for him are consistent with his age, stage of development, and individual ability. Know your son and know what is realistic to expect from him.

So, my dear fellow mother of boys, my advice to you is to learn to love and embrace the busyness, the chaos, the activity, and the energy. All those things are a part of your son. See them as the gifts they truly are. Your son is a bundle of potential; point that potential in a positive direction and then let him go for it! Teach him how to harness his own power, and it will serve him well throughout his life.

To close out this chapter, I'd like to share a little story from my own life. Right now, as I write this, I am on a trip with some of my children to visit my grandmother. All but one of my boys is here with me. To get here, we spent 6 hours driving in a car, followed by 45 minutes on a ferry and another 15 minute car ride. By the time we made it to our rental house, the youngest boys were ready to burst with pent up energy. They tumbled out of the car, racing each other for the door. For the next hour, they ran around the house, chasing each other, exploring their new surroundings, and yelling at the top of their lungs. It was utter and complete chaos. By the time bedtime rolled around, I was exhausted and I had a headache. In my younger days, I would have become angry and frustrated with them. I might have even disciplined them or reprimanded them. But the wisdom of decades of experience in mothering boys has taught me that the more I try to reign them in during a circumstance like this, the more their energy will fight for an outlet, and the more destructive they will become. I knew that if I let them get some of those pent up wiggles and noise out now, they would be happier and better prepared for bedtime when it rolled around. And that's just what happened. I suggested they run around outside for a bit, which they happily did. Then, we went through our bedtime routine, snuggled down into bed, and they were fast asleep (and so was I!) before they knew it. The next morning dawned with renewed energy for both the boys and their mama, but everyone was happy and excited for what the new day would bring. No regrets for me, and only happy memories for my sons.

Dear fellow mom, please strive with me to live without regrets.

# CHAPTER FOUR

## Boys and Aggression

They hit, they punch, they kick, they run at each other. They posture for the upper hand. They position themselves. It all comes so naturally and easily.

What makes boys so aggressive? Studies show that testosterone, the hormone most predominate in males, is closely linked to aggression.[8] Testosterone is directly responsible for inducing competitive and even criminal behavior.

Is there something deeper going on here? Is there more of a reason for this than simply that males like to fight one another to become top dog? And if so, why do these tendencies start so young?

Throughout the years of raising my boys, I've often wondered why they have such strong aggressive tendencies. Why do they fight so easily, and how are they able to move on from it so quickly afterwards? What is it in boys that makes them want to hit and punch and shove, even from the time they are toddlers?

Though I'll never understand the reasoning behind their tendencies toward aggression, I have come to accept and appreciate that it is part of who they are. There is a very specific reason why boys are designed to be more aggressive that girls.

Boys' tendency toward aggression really goes back to the primary way with which they tend to interact with the world. They are more physically oriented, and so they interact in a more physical nature. Their rough and tumble approach to life is evidence of this more physical orientation to their environment.

Despite what many moms (and others) believe, the aggressiveness typical of boys' behavior is normal and natural. That's not to say that it is acceptable in every situation. But knowing it is normal can help ease a mom's mind. No, you are not raising a psychopath just because your little boy likes to punch and wrestle. Obviously, boys need to learn appropriate ways to express this aggression, which includes, in most cases, not punching and wrestling. Even those types of activities have their place in specific situations, which we will discuss more in a few moments.

In all actuality, this aggressiveness may serve a very important purpose. It is no accident that most boys tend to be this way. In the mind of your little boy, he is learning how to establish his place in the world. He is learning how to do what the Bible calls "taking dominion." In Genesis, when God created the first man and woman and placed them in the garden of Eden, He told them to be fruitful and multiply and take dominion over the earth. And again, when the earth was flooded and only eight people were saved, God told Noah and his sons and their wives to be fruitful and take dominion over all the earth. He has never rescinded that command. It is still our duty as humans to take dominion over the earth, to be stewards over and care for God's creation. Men are particularly equipped to conquer, master, and steward resources and situations in order to best utilize them, and this is evidenced early in their development.

We can also think of this concept of taking dominion as "claiming territory." Boys and men have a need and desire to conquer something. They find fulfillment through overcoming obstacles and subduing opposition. They want to succeed at silencing their critics. They often feel they have something to prove to themselves and others.

Aggression does not have to express itself in offensive or harmful ways. It is possible for boys to be kind and considerate while still expressing a more forward moving or aggressive nature. Tackling and overcoming a challenge is an ideal way to channel a more aggressive approach to life. "Taking the bull by the horns" is a perfect word picture to describe how this can play out in a boy or man's life.

**How do I handle it?**

As moms what can we do to help our boys direct these feelings and tendencies in healthy and productive ways while simultaneously teaching them it is wrong to harm or take advantage of others?

## Teach them to be protectors

First, it is essential that we begin teaching our sons very early on that they have a job to protect and defend those who are weaker than them or need their help. Knowing someone else depends on him to keep them safe will give a boy a sense of worth and value like few other things in life can. They have a God given instinct to protect whatever is under their care. Nurture and encourage that instinct. This will raise up a heart of compassion in them and give them the ability to more effectively direct their aggressive tendencies.

Even when they are as young as toddler and preschool age, talk about the way a gentleman is supposed to treat others. Make this way of thinking such a part of everyday conversation that your son has no excuse for not knowing the polite, honorable, kind way to behave in any situation. As they grow older, continue to emphasize the importance of putting other people first. Encourage them to look for ways to serve both individuals and also within their community. Teach them the concept of loving their neighbor. Remember, however, that the way a boy shows love may not look the same as the way you would show love. He's probably not going to be going around hugging everyone (although if he does, that's great!), but he may display love with acts of service. Doing something for someone else may be how he shows love and compassion.

Kindness is something everyone should practice, no matter

their gender. Show your sons an example of kindness and consideration for others. Introduce them to other men who exemplify kindness and compassion, whether men in their own lives like their dads, grandfathers, uncles, and friends, or historical figures they meet through books. There are plenty to choose from. Just be sure these examples display the kind of love and consideration you want your son to have while still being able to accomplish important things with their lives.

Expect your boy to treat you like a lady. Show him how a gentleman acts toward a lady and require him to treat you that way. Have your son, even at a young age, open the door for you and others. Instruct him on how to give up his seat for a lady or an elderly person. Direct him toward opportunities to help an older person or a young mother with carrying a heavy item. Start this at home with your family. Emphasize how he should treat women (mom and sisters) and children (younger siblings) with respect and protectiveness. Instill in him a sense of honor for the elderly and handicapped. Teach him the gentlemanly arts are that being lost in our culture of selfishness today. Draw out these God-given instincts of manly protectiveness in your son. Encourage this considerate, protective behavior in him, and those aggressive tendencies will not end up being misused to bring harm to others.

**Help them to be productive**

Second, give them chances to use this tendency toward a more aggressive approach to life in productive and constructive ways. Men and boys like to fix and create things. Whether it's building a ship with legos or designing a computer program or repairing an engine, they want to be doing. Why not teach them to use that desire to their advantage to accomplish something worthwhile?

You can help your son learn early on how to effectively channel his energies into useful pursuits by giving him lots of age appropriate opportunities to master and overcome challenges. For a toddler, building a tower with blocks is a challenge to master. For a preschool age boy, building roads in the sandbox with his toy cars can give him an outlet for this urge toward mastering something. Older boys might enjoy sports or other outdoor activities. Most boys like to build things with their hands. Seek out ways for them to learn how. Give them chores to be responsible for and emphasize how important it is for the rest of the family that he fulfills his duty. Let him know that other people are depending on him to take out the trash, or shovel the walkway, or feed the dog (or whatever chore you deem appropriate for his age and abilities). Tell him regularly in a positive and encouraging way that his contribution to the family is very important and that you are proud of him when he is responsible and reliable in completing his chores. This will do wonders for him. Boys want to feel useful and needed. You, mom, can help him have that, not through false praise, but in response to him accomplishing a useful and necessary task that brings benefit to the whole family.

Boys need to feel needed. Give them something worthwhile to do.

**They need projects**

Beyond household chores, boys need important projects that challenge them and force them to work and to grow as people. They need circumstances in their lives that will make them have to dig deep to find what it takes to accomplish their goal. Life is full of these kinds of opportunities. As moms, we want to shelter our children and protect them from anything that might be hard. Although I know it can be difficult to see your baby struggle with something difficult, don't make everything in life easy for them. Struggle often produces character. That's not to say that you should allow your son to be endangered or risk his injury. We do have an obligation to keep our children safe from harmful situations. We should never endanger our children for the sake of teaching them a lesson. They are depending on us for their personal safety, and we must preserve that at all costs. What I do mean is that often we make things easier for our children than they have to be. Many moms do everything for their children, never requiring them to pitch in and help out in any way. This is doing a great disservice to our children.

Boys need to develop confidence and fortitude. How will they be able to do that if they are never allowed to do anything?

I recently heard about a fifteen-year-old boy whose mother would not allow him to light a match because she didn't trust him to do it safely. How in the world, in just three short years from now, will this boy be able to live on his own and function in life without basic knowledge such as how to light a match? Guiding our sons in learning life skills like these at age-appropriate times is essential in preparing them for real life beyond the four walls of our home. When we trust our sons to learn new skills when they are ready, we demonstrate to them that they are worthy of our trust. Children live up to the expectations we place upon them. If we expect our children to be irresponsible and unable to do difficult things, that is what they will become. In our culture today, we have an epidemic of young people who do not know how to do the most basic skills in life.

The idea of "adulting" has come about because so many young people simply have not been taught basic life skills like laundry and paying bills, and so it has become an insurmountable task to operate as an adult, even as a person in their early twenties. What a shame. Young mother, don't make the same mistake so many in my generation of mothers has done. Don't over shelter your children (sons and daughters) from the difficult things in life. Let them try to do hard things and get the sense of accomplishment that comes from succeeding at something hard.

But, you say, what if they don't succeed? Let them feel failure, too. Failure is one of life's best teachers. We learn a lot from failure. With you by his side, encouraging and giving wisdom, your son will not be overcome by his failures. Show him how to embrace and learn from failure, then how to get back up and try again. True success in life often only comes from learning from our mistakes and trying again until we get it right. Give your son the opportunity to learn this lesson early in life in a safe and loving environment with the encouragement and support you can give him. He will thank you some day.

## The positive side of aggression

Aggression in boys does not automatically mean your son is a social miscreant or that he is destined for a life of crime. Aggressive tendencies can actually be channeled into productive pursuits. Harness that aggression, encourage it to develop in healthier directions, and challenge your son to use his energy and abilities to help and serve others. Your son is a potentially powerful force for good in this world. Show him how to be one—show him you believe in him and trust him to do important and helpful things.

Politeness, kindness, compassion for others, a willingness to help, and a determination to succeed can all spring from the root of aggressive tendencies—if those tendencies are carefully and deliberately directed toward good and positive means of expression.

# CHAPTER FIVE

## Boys and Entertainment

No matter where you look, it's hard to escape the fact that we are an entertainment saturated culture. We spend much of our free time in passively and often mindlessly allowing ourselves to be entertained. It's such a part of who we are as a people that anyone who does not, for instance, own a TV is considered culturally backward and socially inept.

Entertainment is such a part of our culture that as parents, how we handle entertainment in regards to our children has become a huge part of our responsibilities. We are faced with the burden of how best to approach things like TV, the internet, video games, social media, movies, music, sports, books, and other forms of entertainment.

How do we make decisions when faced with so many choices and so many areas requiring our oversight? And if we decide based on what we think is best, will we be swimming upstream against the cultural norms? How will that affect our children?

When it comes to the question of entertainment in how we raise our boys, we are met with some serious challenges. There are so many questions that need to be answered, so many decisions that need to be made, and so many approaches to be considered, it is a topic that can quickly become overwhelming.

There is so much we need to inform ourselves about and so many topics to address when thinking of our sons and the entertainment they are exposed to. It's dizzying to keep up with all the technological changes we encounter in today's world. Where do we turn, and how do we know what sources of information to trust? How can we find out what really is the best way to handle entertainment in our sons' lives?

There are several areas to consider when discussing our boys and how they spend their free time. Let's break it down and talk about each area.

**Sports**

I realize my personal opinion and the choices we have made as a family may go against the societal norm, but I am going to share my position and hopefully give encouragement to other moms out there who, like me, feel like they are swimming upstream when it comes to the topic of boys and organized sports.

Sports can be a fun and healthy outlet for boys' energy

and aggression. Learning to work with others in a team setting, developing determination, experiencing both wins and losses, opportunities to learn good sportsmanship, and setting and reaching goals can all be ways in which participating in sports can be beneficial. It can be a great experience and kids who play sports often have wonderful memories and even develop some good character traits as a result.

I am in no way against playing or watching organized sports. However, I believe there is a tendency in our culture to elevate sports and sports figures to a status that can lead to an unhealthy focus on sports, to the exclusion of other more important or useful areas of life. I see so many young men who have spent many hours of their lives plunked down on a couch, a bowl of nachos in their hands, yelling at a TV screen, and thinking they've really done something with their time, when all they've actually done is watch someone else play a game for several hours.

There's nothing wrong with watching sports, but when it becomes an obsession or an excuse to escape from more productive pursuits, it can become detrimental. We need to teach our boys to keep entertainment, including sports, in balance with the rest of their lives. There is a time and a place for sports games, whether watching or playing, and there is a time for more serious or valuable uses for our time. Unless your son is a particularly gifted athlete who has a surefire chance at playing professional sports, time spent on developing sports related skills should be balanced with time spent on developing skills that will be useful in his everyday life.

Camaraderie and exercise are good reasons to involve boys in sports activities, but again, keep it in perspective. Weigh heavily how much time you want your son to invest into activities that may be fun and help pass the time, but most likely won't have lasting value in his adult life someday.

When it comes to boys and sports, keep it in perspective. Remember to look at the bigger picture. If your son finds playing sports a fun way to spend his free time, by all means encourage him to participate. If it is interfering with his studies or the day to day functioning of the household, it may be time to step back and reevaluate the importance of continuing that particular activity.

I know a lot of moms who spend a lot of time sitting on bleachers and in driver's seats to accommodate some ideal of the perfect mom as one who has her kids in many activities, shuttling them from one sports practice to another. The kids are exhausted, mom is exhausted, nobody's happy, they eat most of their weekday meals in the car en route to yet another event. What lasting value is there in this type of upbringing for those children? Will our sons really benefit from an unbalanced emphasis such as that?

Sports can be a great use of free time for boys. They can also be a huge distraction from more important uses of their time. The key to balance in this area is to keep the bigger picture in perspective. Ask yourself, "How does being involved in this activity make my son a better person? How will it help him to develop into the man he needs to be to be successful and serve God more effectively in life?" The answers to those questions will give the clues needed to make the decision about whether being involved in a particular sports activity is right for your son.

## TV and Movies

Twelve years ago, my husband and I decided to get rid of our TV access. It's been one of the best decisions we ever made for our family. Honestly, we found ourselves wasting so much time watching TV that getting rid of it was incredibly freeing. There was too much temptation to waste time or to watch things we probably shouldn't—getting rid of it made things much simpler by taking the temptation away.

I'm not saying everyone should get rid of their TV. There are some helpful and interesting programs on TV. It can be a great way to learn new information and at times a harmless way to pass some time. However, just as it was for us, it can be a huge time waster. With regards to families with young children, it can be a means of exposure to all kinds of content most responsible parents don't want their kids to see.

Regarding both TV and movies, be cautious about what your sons are viewing. Choose the shows and movies they watch carefully (and don't forget about the commercials). Know what your son is watching. Even seemingly innocent kids' shows can sometimes contain subject matter that many parents would deem inappropriate for their children to see. Don't be afraid to censor what they watch; it's part of your job as a mom.

As parents we should also be concerned not just with the content of what our children are watching or with the time wasting aspect of it, but also with the fact that watching something on a screen is a purely passive activity. When we are watching TV or movies, we're not actually doing anything. And yet, somehow we often feel as though we have done something. It's a strange dichotomy. Be very careful and aware of just how much time your son spends in front of a screen on any given day. Studies have shown that the average American child between the ages of 2 and 11 spends up to twenty-four hours in front of the TV per week.[9] That's a lot of time spent not doing anything productive. It's no wonder, with statistics like that, we have an obesity epidemic in our country. There are a lot of people, young children included, not doing much moving around for a large part of their day.

Studies have also shown that excessive TV viewing can be detrimental to brain development in young children.[10] As human beings, we are meant to be moving and doing, not passively sitting for extended periods of time. Get your son outside. Encourage him to engage in active play. Don't let him waste his life staring at a screen.

**Video games**

Just like with TV and movies, video games can be a huge time waster for boys. There is an addictive nature to video games that can suck boys in. Many boys spend hours a day playing video games, at the exclusion of other more socially interactive or health promoting activities. For very similar reasons as with TV and movie viewing, parents must be very cautious and aware of the games their sons are playing and exactly how much time they spend playing them.

An even bigger concern with video games is the violent nature of the games themselves. As discussed in a previous chapter, boys have a tendency toward aggression. Rather than detracting from this aggressive tendency or channeling it in a more constructive direction, violent video games feed this aggression. Studies have shown that playing violent video games can lead to violent behavior in real life.[11] These games tend to desensitize the players to acts of violence to the extent that they often show no remorse when acting out their aggression on real life victims. It does not seem to register in their brains that reality is different than the games taking place behind a screen.

I realize not all, or even most of the boys (and young men) who play violent video games will go on to commit acts of violence on others. But there does seem to be a correlation between certain tendencies toward violent behavior and video game usage. When it comes to our sons and violent video games, isn't it better to be safe than sorry?

## The Internet

The internet is an indescribably useful tool and also an inexplicably dangerous frontier, filled with traps and pitfalls for anyone not cautious and aware of the dangers. It behooves us as parents of sons to inform ourselves of the danger and take measures to protect and instruct our sons accordingly.

Pornography and online predators are real dangers facing our boys every time they turn on a computer or pick up a smartphone. Young boys are often a target of evil people who wish to take advantage of our sons' innocence and steal it from them in horrifying ways. They lurk in the shadows of the internet's darker side and lay wait for our boys, who often stumble upon them by accident. Statistics show that 93% of young boys have been exposed to pornography on the internet during their adolescence. The average age at which a boy is first exposed to online pornography is age 11.[12] Those are some shocking numbers. As mothers, this kind of thing causes us great concern. But what can we do about it? How can we fight more effectively for the innocence and purity of our sons?

Though controlling or limiting our sons' internet usage is challenging, it is not impossible. There are plenty of effective filters and safety measures that can be used to keep it under parents' control. These can be very effective and I would highly recommend researching and investing in these tools for your family's protection. However, nothing is foolproof. A multi-pronged approach to this issue is by far the most effective approach.

Set up other safeguards in the home. Don't allow young boys to use the internet unsupervised. Set time limits on internet usage. Install passwords. Use software that tracks every site visited on a particular computer or device.

Beyond these measures, and more importantly, talk from a young age with your boys about the dangers of the internet. Instill in them from early on a desire to keep their hearts and minds pure from corrupting images and activities. Know who your son's friends are and how they spend their time together. Develop a close relationship with your son, one in which he not only feels comfortable talking with you about his thoughts and concerns, but also one in which disappointing you would cause him great sadness and pain. Build a relationship wherein there is so much respect for you on the part of your son that he would never dream of doing something he would be ashamed of if you knew about it.

Most importantly, enforce in your son a sense of the omnipresence and omniscience of God. That's just the fancy theological terms often used to say that God is everywhere, can see everything we do, and know what is going on in our hearts and minds. Keeping secrets from other people, including parents, may mean a young boy can get away with something in terms of parental consequences, but he must develop an understanding that there are no secrets from God. He sees and knows it all and we aren't getting away with anything in regards to Him.

As seriously as we take our responsibility to protect our sons, and as many measures as we may take to keep them safe, by far the most important safeguard we can have in place is a son with a conscience that is sensitive toward God and knowledge that he is accountable to God for his actions and the choices he makes.

**Social media**

To some degree, social media could fall under the heading

of internet usage. However, it deserves a category of its own here mainly because it is growing and changing so rapidly; it presents challenges of its own. Social media is an interesting beast. With the constant updates made to social media platforms and the sheer number of those platforms available today, a responsible parent is hard pressed to keep up with everything happening at any given time in the world of social media. Cyber bullying, "sexting," online predators, and inappropriate content are just a few of the areas of concern we face as parents in regards to our sons's use of social media.

I may be a bit of a dinosaur when I share this opinion, and you are welcome to disagree, but limiting the age at which our children are allowed to use social media is a wise course of action, I believe. Most children under the age of 13 or 14 don't have the discernment yet to wisely handle access to social media. You are more than welcome to disagree with me here. However, my philosophy when it comes to this matter is "better safe than sorry." Social media, like TV, movies, and video games, can be a huge time waster. Unlike other forms of digital entertainment, however, it's much easier to waste large amounts of time without realizing it or knowing where that time "disappeared" to.

You are not a bad parent if you limit your son's time spent on social media. In fact, it can be a loving and responsible thing as a mom to keep a handle on your son's social media use. Don't be afraid to be in charge in this area. Help your son develop good habits regarding social media.

**Keep entertainment in its place**

When thinking through the choices before us regarding how our boys spend their free time, there are a lot of things to consider. Weigh carefully the benefits and detriments of any activity and make informed decisions. Be proactive in how you handle these decisions. Choose to be intentional and purposeful in directing how your son uses his leisure hours. You will be helping him develop habits and appetites for the future—make sure they are a good use of the time he has available to him throughout his life.

A balanced approach to entertainment is important for your son's future success.

# CHAPTER SIX

This chapter will be a brief one, but I wanted to touch on boys and friendships, and I felt that topic needed a chapter of its own.

**Boys and friends**

The Bible discusses in many places the importance of choosing the right friends. We should never underestimate the power a choice in friends can have to the direction of a person's life. Every one of us is greatly affected (more than we even realize or are perhaps willing to admit) by the people with whom we spend our time.

Here are just a few passages of Scripture which refer to friendships and the impact they have on our lives.[13]

> Whoever walks with the wise becomes wise, but the companion of fools will suffer harm.
> Proverbs 13:20

Faithful are the wounds of a friend; profuse are the kisses of an enemy.
Proverbs 27:6

Oil and perfume make the heart glad, and the sweetness of a friend comes from his earnest counsel. Do not forsake your friend and your father's friend, and do not go to your brother's house in the day of your calamity.
Proverbs 27:9-10

Iron sharpens iron, and one man sharpens another.
Proverbs 27:17

The one who keeps the law is a son with understanding, but a companion of gluttons shames his father.
Proverbs 28:7

Knowing how much friendships can affect us all in general, shouldn't we as moms of boys be especially concerned with whom our sons choose as their friends?

Who we choose to spend our time with has a direct effect on who we are as a person. It has been said that we become like the five people we hang around with the most. This is even more true of young people who are still developing and do not yet have a sense of their own identity.

What kind of people do you allow your son to spend time with? Who are his closest friends? Are they the sort of people you want your son to become like? Be aware, dear mother, of who your son's friends are.

One of my sons was a part of a particular group of young boys at one time. Whenever he spent time with these boys, he seemed to get himself into trouble. Yet, the other boys never seemed to. We found out after some time that often my son was blamed for the wrongdoing of another member of the group, and because of his easygoing personality, he ended up as the scapegoat. Friends can make you or break you, as my son could attest.

Help your son choose his friends. Don't be afraid to set limits on your son's social interactions. When children are young, this can be easily done. As they get older, however, it becomes increasingly difficult to control the kinds of friends your son chooses. That's why it's extremely important to develop a close relationship with your son, so that he will naturally look to you for guidance and wisdom when making choices in his companions.

We've all heard stories of good kids who got involved with the wrong crowd. It never turns out well for the good, decent kids. Somehow, they always end up in trouble or getting blamed for things the others did. "Guilty by association" often applies in those types of situations. Be on guard and protect your son from ending up in a position like that.

Often, when asked why their lives ended up the way they did, prison inmates will say it can be attributed to a poor choice of companions. They often regret the friends they chose more than many other decisions, because that choice was the catalyst to the other, increasingly worse, choices they made along the way toward their personal downfall.

Along this line of thought, it's essential that we teach our sons how to stand firm in what is right, even when everyone around them is doing the wrong thing. Having a clear grasp of right and wrong and a conscience which is sensitive and responsive is so very important.

Lay a foundation for your son of how to choose good friends who will have a beneficial influence on him. Show him how having good friends can challenge him toward being a better person. Warn him of the dangers of poor choices in friends. This kind of instruction will be vital to his later success and happiness in life.

# CHAPTER SEVEN

Educating boys is a topic often misunderstood and fraught with challenges. In today's culture, students who sit quietly and learn in a more auditory or visually based style are considered good students. Those who learn by doing and experiencing are considered flawed or unintelligent. Yet, the ones who learn in more hands on ways are the ones who are often the innovators and creatives. They are the ones who, now in their early twenties up into their thirties, are leading the way in developing technology and finding new ways of doing things. They promise to be the valuable players in the coming future.

Boys, as we have discussed in a previous chapter, are often more active than girls. That doesn't mean that all boys are constantly moving. It also doesn't mean that all girls sit quietly for hours on end. There are differences in personality and expression, of course. However, there are a disproportionate number of boys who are considered "too active" for the classroom setting.

As we discussed in the chapter on boys and energy levels, boys have a harder time being still and quiet for long periods of time. It is unreasonable to expect them to be able to do so for 6 or 8 hours every day. Many behavioral issues facing modern parents in regards to their boys' behavior are directly connected to the fact that boys are active and need to be able to move regularly. Isn't it interesting that a larger number of boys are diagnosed with ADHD, at a much higher percentage than girls? Often, boys are given this label simply because they are active little boys. They are often prescribed medication to "fix" the "problem," when all along there is not really anything wrong with them at all. They are just being normal boys.

Classroom settings are notoriously ill-suited for the natural expression of little boys' energy levels. Children are often expected to sit and listen and observe, rarely being required or allowed to actively participate in what is happening. As a result, they fidget, they lose interest, and they act bored or misbehave. Then, they are labelled. This label follows them and often defines them throughout their school years.

What a shame that we have stifled the activity, creativity, curiosity, and even genius of a generation of little boys. These boys have so much potential, and we have squashed it with our unrealistic expectations. When they don't meet those expectations, we medicate them, further stifling them and making them feel as though there is something in them that is flawed and inadequate. We send them the message that who they are is wrong— that they need to take a pill to make them more acceptable to society.

What a disservice we do to our sons and to ourselves when we approach the situation this way. We would be much better served to come up with educational alternatives which value the differences in all of our children and celebrate the amazing potential in our sons.

How can we manage and direct our boys' attention so they can get the maximum benefit from their education? How can we value their active natures while still teaching them the skills they need and giving them the education which will best benefit them? This is not an easy question in today's culture. In our current educational system, it can be very challenging to find ways to value yet still effectively instruct our boys.

It boils down to a philosophy of education. If you believe that our children's minds are buckets to fill with information, the ideal scenario is for those little buckets to be open and receptive to everything you dump into them. However, if you believe that human beings are designed with an innate desire to learn, uniquely expressed in each person, that is evident from birth, you understand that the most effective approach to education is to stir that instinctive thirst for knowledge all children have. You then see that by primarily encouraging the child to love learning, you are approaching education in the most effective manner. A child who loves to learn will be an interested and engaged student.

The trouble comes with the fact that the typical classroom setting is based on the former philosophy, rather than the later. Classrooms are designed for a teacher to stand in front of a number of students and pour out information, which presumably will land into the minds of those students and stay there. But what if the second philosophy is more accurate? What happens to these students then? Their natural thirst for knowledge is often squelched by the traditional classroom approach. What could have had the potential to capture their interest and imagination becomes boring and uninteresting, and they soon tune it out. They have not been challenged to engage with the information in a way that incorporates their whole being. The information has been force fed to them, and they begin to choke on it. It is not always the fault of the teachers. It is certainly not the fault of the students. Rather, it is a major flaw in the typical educational system itself. There is an error in the philosophy that undergirds the system.

For some students, this system of education works because of the way they are naturally designed to learn. They are more visually oriented, therefore passively reading or listening to someone present information is the primary way in which they learn. Some students learn in spite of the system, not necessarily because of it. However, it does a disservice to all students because it treats them as empty receptacles, rather than living, growing, spiritual beings with souls and minds that need to be nurtured and treated with respect.

What is the solution to this dilemma?

**Two kinds of educational approaches**

For our family, the obvious choice of educational method is homeschooling. Homeschooling is steadily gaining in popularity. The number of families choosing to homeschool is continuing to grow each year.[14] One reason many families are choosing to homeschool is because homeschooling offers a chance to give a child an education specifically tailored to their strengths and learning style.

Homeschool families with boys have the flexibility to work with the boys' energy levels, interests, and abilities. It is generally more unusual for a homeschooled boy, especially one who has been educated at home from early on, to be diagnosed with ADHD. Homeschooled students, whether boys or girls, tend to do better academically overall.[15]

Homeschooling gives families the flexibility to cater to the needs of each individual child in the home. Have a wiggly little boy who has a hard time paying attention? Keep the lessons short, interesting, and active. There is more than one way to skin a cat, as they say. Studying history, for example, doesn't have to be boring. It can be fun by doing activities that bring it to life. When my older boys were little, our homeschooling included a lot of dressing up and playacting. My oldest son loved to first learn about a particular time period in history, then collect objects he could combine into a costume depicting that time period. He would then act out scenes revolving around the things he had learned in our history study. As an adult, history is one of his many passions. He is continually learning new things, and his hunger to learn more about history is insatiable. I am absolutely astounded at times at the extent of the information he knows about people, places, and events in history. I would consider myself a history buff as well, but the vastness of his knowledge far surpasses mine. I cannot lay claim to having passed down to him all the information he now possesses. The only credit I can claim is that I didn't squash his early interest in the subject. He had plenty of room to learn and explore and expand his understanding on his own terms. That is the freedom homeschooling affords.

My second oldest son is mechanically minded. From a very young age, he has instinctively known how machines work. He has a talent for working with his hands, and a determination to learn whatever he sets his mind on. At the age of 17 he has already started two successful businesses of his own and has also made himself an extremely valuable employee in the business for which he works part time. This young man is a natural-born entrepreneur. Because he has been free to pursue his slightly out of the box interests, he is excelling and already knows where he wants to go in life. He knows what he wants, and he has a well-laid plan for how to achieve it. How many young men in their late teens can say that? Very few, I would venture to guess. Again, I cannot take any of the credit for the impressive talents my son has shown at such a young age. His father and I merely gave him opportunities to develop his talents and the free time to pursue his interests.

I have known many young men like my sons who have had a jump start in life because of their experiences with homeschooling. There is a young man in our church who, because of a good work ethic and an early start in employment is on the fast track to management in retail at the young age of 24. I know young men who have started their own film production companies and created award-winning movies in their late teens and early twenties. My husband has mentored young men interested in woodworking, one of whom at just 20 years old started his own very successful cabinetmaking business. When we give our boys the space and time they need and look for the opportunities, the sky is the limit on what these young men can (and will) achieve. Never underestimate the power of a flexible education tailored to the interest and abilities of the specific student.

For too long, we have placed limits on our boys. We have tried to force them into a box. We have told them that learning to sit quietly and getting good grades in school is more important that living boldly and trying new things. They need the freedom to explore and do and experiment and grow.

What does this kind of freedom look like when you are in the trenches with a squirmy, active little boy who can't seem to pay attention to his lessons? My third son, who is by far my most distractible of all of my children, is a good example of a boy with a lot of future potential that needs some special care and attention in order to nurture that potential into something worthwhile and amazing. He has a hard time remembering what he has been sent to retrieve, even when he has only moved one room away to get said item. A daily assignment in math, one of his stronger subjects, can either take only minutes or 2 hours for him to complete, depending on how well he is paying attention at the time. There is no doubt in my mind he would not survive in a classroom setting. He would most likely be diagnosed as having ADHD. Maybe he does. But I will never let something like that define him. Rather, he is my highly imaginative, curious, scientifically mind-ed boy who wants to know how everything (and I mean everything!) works. He will patiently watch a caterpillar crawl along a leaf for 20 minutes without moving, but he can't seem to sit still at the dinner table to save his life. Is there something wrong with him? Absolutely not! He is just a very wonderful, specially gifted child whose mind works in a unique and wonderful way. God has given him a brilliant mind and a love of the natural world. He is my little scientist. Only God knows yet what He has planned for my boy, but I certainly don't want to be the one who stands in his way.

Your son is uniquely gifted as well. He, just like my sons, has special talents and abilities to develop. He has a special gift to offer to the world. Don't let his school experience stand in the way of him developing those gifts and talents. Give him opportunities and the freedom to learn and grow and love the world around him.

Beatrix Potter once famously said, "Thank goodness I was never sent to school; it would have rubbed off some of the originality." I think this sentiment can be applied to most creative people. Be very careful to not rub off any of your own son's uniqueness.

When boys are little, it's important to keep their school lessons short and to the point. Never give a little boy busy work. Don't assign a ton of "seat work" such as fill in the blanks worksheets and lots of tests. These types of assignments don't have any real educational value (especially for younger children) and really just serve to make your kids hate schoolwork. Read aloud to your son—a lot. And while you are reading aloud, don't expect him to sit quietly with his hands folded in his lap. Let him play with blocks or color a picture. Though it seems counterintuitive, keeping his hands busy will help him be able to pay attention more closely. It gives him something to channel his energy into so that his mind is freed up to listen and take in what you are reading to him.

Whenever possible, incorporate something hands-on into your schoolwork. Use manipulatives when doing math problems. Do science experiments. Practice spelling words on a big white board so he can make large movements while he writes.

As I mentioned in a previous chapter, boys' fine motor skills tend to develop later than girls'. Boys often have a hard time with the physical act of writing. Try to keep the time they spend writing to a minimum, at least when they are very young. If your son complains that his hand hurts from writing, believe him and switch to a different subject that doesn't require writing. You can always go back to the writing when his hand has had a break. Take your son's physical design into account and make learning a more pleasant experience for both of you.

Get outside together. Go for nature walks. Act out scenes from a favorite book. Take a field trip to a local zoo. Go to the library. Think of creative ideas which you can implement to make your school time more active and interesting to your son. Learning should be fun!

**Traditional school**

Perhaps you are thinking, "That's fine for you. You are already homeschooling your sons. But I can't do that." Not every family will choose to homeschool. Not every mom has the option to stay home with her kids and teach them herself. And that's okay. With some effort and dedication, you can help your son reach his full potential and enjoy learning. It will take some work on your part. I know you want what is best for your son, or you wouldn't be reading this book.

I sympathize with you. I know how hard it is to want the best for your son and feel like the resources available to you are limited.

Or maybe you believe that a traditional school setting really is the best approach to education. That's okay, too. I hope, however, that you will at least consider that a typical classroom setting does present challenges for boys that need to be addressed.

Knowing that boys have a tendency to be more active and that their natural curiosity and interest in learning is often dampened by being in a classroom environment, how can we best serve our sons who must take part in this type of educational situation? This question does not have an easy answer.

The most important thing we can do as mothers of boys is help them understand the worth and value they have as human beings made in the image of God. They need to know how important and worthy they are and that they have been made for a specific purpose in life. They must be reminded regularly that they have a valuable place in this world and that they have been given special talents and gifts to help them better fill that place. Whether in a traditional school setting or homeschool, these truths, when embraced by our sons, will give them the courage and direction to pursue their callings in life and grow into the men God intends them to be. Instill a sense of belonging and worth in your son, and he will be able to overcome any obstacle he may face.

One practical way you can help your son thrive in the classroom is to help his teachers understand how boys and girls are different. Give your child's teachers access to information that will arm them with the knowledge to help them appreciate they way boys are made. Doing this will help not just your own son, but many other boys as well. With this knowledge, your son's teachers will be able to understand and work with a wide variety of students in the most effective way.

When your son is outside of the classroom, give him a chance to run and move and use that boundless energy. Get him involved in active pursuits that direct his energy in positive ways. This will help him be able to be more focused when it's school time. Give him the freedom to play and explore and feed his natural curiosity. Show interest in the things that interest him. Talk to him about his rock collection or his latest lego creation or how his baseball practice went. Encourage him to pursue things he intrigued by. Take him to the library and read a book together on a topic he wants to know more about. Invest in your son; it will come back a hundredfold in the kind of person your son will someday become.

**A few more thoughts on education**

Whether you choose to homeschool or send your son into a traditional school setting, his success is directly linked to your involvement in his education. Encourage in him a love of learning. Stir up his natural interests and talents and give him an opportunity to develop them. He will grow as a person and in his knowledge and understanding of the world around him as you involve yourself in his educational experience. It is more than worth the time and attention you choose to invest in your son and his education. Someday he will thank you for taking the time and interest to help him become all he is meant to be.

# CHAPTER EIGHT

**R-E-S-P-E-C-T: Moms, boys, and the "R" word**

Having now gone through the raising of two teenaged boys, I can say that as a mom, respect from your grown son is something you have to earn, not just demand. I say that slightly tongue-in-check. However, when I was a young mom with a couple of little boys, I had no idea how essential it would be to understand the issue of respect. I thought if I just taught my boys how to obey what I told them to do, respect for me would soon follow. I have found that is not necessarily to case.

Teaching your son to respect you and others is an important and often challenging task. It is, however essential for a healthy and strong mother-son relationship. Boys need to learn how to show respect to others, and this learning must start at a young age.

**Give them an example**

What is the most effective way of instilling a sense of respect in our sons? We as moms must model the type of respect we want to see in our sons. Showing respect for our husbands and others in authority is an important way to give our sons the example they need to see in us. When we are respectful to those we ourselves answer to, no matter the circumstance, our sons will see that respect modeled for them in healthy and appropriate ways. It will send them a signal that it is acceptable and normal (and even desirable in many cases) for each of us to be under authority.

We are all, as God's creation, subject to His authority before all others. Our sons must come to a clear understanding of the authority of God over their lives. Leading them to embrace that authority of God over them will be a major asset to them as they move through their lives, and especially as they face various temptations and trials. Rebellion against God's authority over them will lead them into all kinds of trouble and heartache. Therefore, instilling in them a reverence for God is an essential aspect of their upbringing. We as mothers must not neglect to guide our sons into a respect and reverence for God's authority. That is the root from which all other respect springs.

When we have a proper respect for God's authority, we will then find it easier to have respect for other forms of authority in our lives. We want our sons to respect their fathers and us, the police, teachers, pastors, and other leaders in their lives. Respect is an essential ingredient in any well-ordered society. By showing them how to show respect, they will grow up knowing in a matter-of-fact way that respect for authority is simply a part of life.

I know I am entering controversial territory with this next point, but it is an important one that I feel needs to be made. As moms of boys, we need to be especially aware of how we treat our husbands (if we are married.) There are several reasons for this, of course, not the least of which is that our boys are watching how we treat their fathers and learning from that. Every day, in how we interact with our husbands, we are showing our sons a picture of what we believe marriage is and of what we believe respect for authority (or lack thereof) show look like. Is that picture a good one, an accurate one, and a God honoring one? Despite how we may personally feel about it, the Bible does say that wives are supposed to show respect to their husbands. "But," you may be saying, "isn't my husband supposed to love me? He doesn't always act all that loving. Why should I have to respect him when he doesn't always behave respectably?" We as wives cannot change our husbands' behaviour. What we can change is our own. We are not accountable for what our husbands do, but we are most assuredly accountable for what we ourselves do. We are told to respect our husbands—no disclaimers, no escape clause. Realistically, an in-depth discussion on this topic would require another entire book. I highly encourage a thorough reading of Emmerson Eggerich's Love and Respect and Martha Peace's The Excellent Wife for further study. Suffice it to say in our present discussion that your son needs to see you respect your husband. Seeing that will give him an idea of not only how he should treat your husband, but also how he should show respect to you as well.

As a mom of a son, be sure you do not neglect this area of your effort to raise your son. It will speak volumes to him about the kind of person you are and the kind of person he should become.

Not only should we as moms model respect to our sons, we should expect respect from them. You may have noticed that I have said several times throughout this book that children often live up to our expectations of them. That is because it is an important concept we all, as parents in particular, and as a society in general need to grasp. When we set an expectation for our sons to show respect to us and others, they will usually reach that expectation. When we expect that they will be disrespectful or rebellious, we shouldn't be surprised when they fulfill that expectation. Don't allow your son to speak to or treat you in a disrespectful way. Boys will come to understand that it is not acceptable to behave this way and will in most cases adjust their behavior accordingly. But this has to start at an early age, even as early as the toddler years. Early training in this regard will go a long way to preventing more serious issues later on in your son's growth.

**Respect for others**

Respect for others is a somewhat rare commodity these days, it seems. So few people seem to respect others' property, space, or viewpoint. Disrespect is rampant across all generations. Young men aren't taught to rise and give their seat to the elderly. No one seems to know how to disagree in a calm and respectful manner, especially on social media. There seems to be very little respect for personal property.

Does it have to be this way? Of course not. Previous generations were taught to show respect to others, no matter their walk or station in life. High regard was shown to the elderly. We can reclaim that lost art of respect by teaching our sons the importance of showing respect to everyone they come upon in life. Mom, it is important that we take it upon ourselves to do this. We as mothers have a great deal of power in this regard. Don't underestimate the influence you can have over your son to teach him to show honor and respect to others. Show him what it means and how to do it.

**Moms respecting their sons**

Now we come to the part that may seem counterintuitive or like it goes against much of what I have already said. But I believe it is an area where many moms of boys, especially as their sons near the teens years, make a mistake. Many moms neglect to understand the importance of showing respect toward their sons.

"Men and boys are far more sensitive, vulnerable, and reactionary to feeling inadequate and disrespected. Sadly, some have profiled these sentiments as rooted in narcissism. But moms know their sons are not egotistical maniacs any more than their daughters are prima donnas for longing to be special, noticed, and loved. A prudent mom gives the benefit of the doubt to her boy. He is a man in the making.

Though we all need love and respect equally, there is a statistically significant gender difference. I asked seven thousand people, 'When in a conflict with your spouse, do you feel unloved or disrespected?' An overwhelming 83 percent of the men said disrespected, and 72 percent of the women said unloved. In other words, quite often during the same conflict, she filters his reaction as unloving and he interprets her reaction as disrespectful.

When a mother and son get into a conflict—a very stressful event to both—the son feels far more disrespected than he feels unloved, and he craves respect more than love. But how many mothers detect this, and if they do, how many know what to say or do? Who has coached a mom to ask, 'Is what I am about to say going to sound respectful or disrespectful to my son?'"[16]

Emerson Eggerich, Mothers & Sons

As Emerson Eggerich points out, just as our husbands need our respect, so do our sons. Showing our sons respect shows them that we care about them as boys and as the men they will someday become.

Boys are very simply men who have not reached maturity. If, as Eggerich asserts, the most important way a man feels valued is by feeling respected, and boys are men not yet fully grown, showing our sons respect is the best way of showing them how much they mean to us.

One of the major challenges we face as moms of boys is not understanding how our sons tick. They just don't make any sense to us sometimes. But we can trust the wisdom that tells us that they need us to respect them. Don't question it; just trust it. Though they cannot articulate this need to us, even in their teenage years, it is a real need. Of course we want to meet their needs as we raise them. And so, we will in turn want to respect them.

How can we show them respect? Eggerich says one of the simplest ways to show respect to our sons is to tell them we respect them. This seems obvious, doesn't It? But I can honestly say that for many years of raising my boys, it never occurred to me to just tell them I respected them. When they do something worthy of respect, point it out, and thank them for it. When they act in an honorable way, mention how proud it makes you. Ask your son's opinion about things. When he shares his opinion, whether asked for or not, don't shoot it down or demean it. Give it thoughtful consideration. If he offers an idea, listen to it and give it weight. When he talks to you about something, take the time to look him in the eye and listen to what he has to say. Show him by your words and actions that what he says and thinks matters to you. Be aware of how you speak to or about him in public; consider his feelings and try to avoid embarrassing him if possible. All these things will speak to his heart in a way that shows that you respect and value him. This will do wonders for his relationship with you, and will ultimately help him become a man who is well worthy of respect throughout his life. You will make him respectable by showing him respect.

Respect can be a difficult area for moms of boys, but with some thoughtful and careful understanding, we can help them learn to respect others and to be respectable themselves. Then they will stand out as rare and worthy individuals in our present culture.

# CHAPTER NINE

**Boys need affection**

Despite how they behave sometimes, boys need us, as their moms, to show affection to them. They may not ask for it, and the affection they need may not look the same as what a daughter may need; nevertheless, boys crave the attention and affection of their mothers. It is often hard for a boy to articulate this need. A lack of attention and affection may manifest itself in other ways, such as acting out, bullying, and other forms of socially inappropriate behavior. These are often born out of a deep frustration, which boys have a difficult time expressing verbally. (Remember back in Chapter 1 when I talked about how boys develop verbal skills later than girls?) Boys often have a hard time putting into words what's going on inside of their hearts and minds. This often leads to them try to express those things in other ways. Watch for signs that your son needs more attention and affection. It will often express itself in anger, frustration, sullenness, or rough treatment of others.

How can we as moms show affection to our sons in ways that speak to their hearts and make them feel loved and valued, and fill that need in them? When our sons are babies and toddlers, it's easy to show them affection. Hugging them, kissing their chubby cheeks, holding their little hands, lifting them up when they reach for us are all natural ways mothers show their love to their children, both boys and girls. One of the wonderful perks of motherhood is the special joy of cuddling our little ones, drinking in the sweetness of their presence and taking in all the little details that make up who they are—their tiny toes, their soft, downy hair, that wonderful baby smell. Giving them affection is simply a part of the privilege and delight of new motherhood.

Maybe, though, you have a baby like my first son, who didn't like to be cuddled. He craved stimulation, and yet was easily overstimulated. He often cried when he held for long periods of time. He still needed my affection and attention. I needed to find a creative way to deliver it that didn't overstimulate him. It can be done. It just takes balance and wisdom and getting to know your child.

Just because they don't ask for affection, doesn't mean boys don't need it. It's one of our main jobs (and joys) as moms to give our boys the affection and attention they need and deserve. As they grow older, they need it even more. They need to know that we like them and enjoy their presence. They need physical contact and the nearness of another human being. They need regular, consistent touch.

Studies show that physical touch is as essential to proper development of children as nourishment.[17] Affection nourishes the soul in the same way that food nourishes the body. Everyone needs it, whether they know it or not.

As boys get older, it becomes less "cool" for boys to receive hugs and similar shows of affection from mom. This doesn't mean that all boys don't need it. They do. We may just need to get creative on the how and when of our shows of affection to our middle school and high school aged sons.

Putting an arm around his shoulder and giving it a squeeze can be a quick and nonintrusive way of showing our teenage sons affection. A high five, a gentle ruffling of the hair, a pat on the back can all be ways to fill that need for affection. It doesn't have to be a big deal; it can be a simple part of everyday life. If it is a natural part of your everyday interaction with your son from the time he is little, he won't resist it when he is older because it might be considered "uncool." He will be happy and grateful for this normal, welcomed display of your love and care for him.

**Many ways to show affection**

There are many different ways you can show affection to your son that go beyond giving him a hug. Be free with your expressions of love and affection from the beginning. So many moms of boys pull back from showing their sons affection when they reach a certain age. Don't make that mistake. Boys of any age need to know their moms love them; show your son you care by showering him with affection.

Hugs are an obvious way to show our boys affection. Studies have shown that just one 30 second hug a day can help dramatically with boosting our mood and improving our health.[18] A simple hug can be a powerful tool. At the end of a long, hard day, nothing soothes quite as much as a long hug from a loved one.

Simple gestures as we pass by or go along our day can convey a sense of care and affection. It doesn't always have to be an elaborate display. Make it a seamless part of your day. Give him a pat on the back when he does something you appreciate, like taking out the trash or mowing the lawn. A squeeze on the shoulder when he says something funny or thoughtful, sitting next to him on the couch as you listen to him tell you about his day, reaching over to pat his knee, and other similar simple gestures can show that you care about him.

When he's sick, it's natural for a mom to want to comfort her son by giving him a back rub or putting a hand on his forehead. It's important to continue to do these things even as he gets older.

**Look at him**

Another perhaps overlooked way we can show affection to our sons is to make eye contact with them throughout the day. Give your son your full attention when he is talking to you. Let him know how important he is to you by looking him straight in the eye and listening carefully to him.

Too many people don't take the time to listen to their children, and then they wonder why their kids don't want to talk to them. Look your son in the eye and let him know you want to hear what he has to say. Eye contact is an excellent way to convey a sense that the other person is important to you in that moment. Look at your son and give him your full, undistracted attention at different times throughout the day.

Make a point to have at least one face-to-face conversation with him each day. It doesn't have to be long; you just have to demonstrate to him that you are paying attention. Don't check your email, don't scroll through Facebook, don't watch TV, don't even chop vegetables for dinner while you mumble "Umm hum" distractedly. Look him in the eye, hear what he is saying, and respond thoughtfully. Do it on a regular basis. This will do more to show your son that he is important to you than almost anything else you may do to build your relationship with him.

**Smile at him**

When was the last time you smiled at your kids? If you can't remember, then you're not smiling often enough. Our facial expressions say a lot about us and what we're thinking. Behavioral scientists estimate that anywhere between 60-90% of communication is nonverbal.[19] What is going on in our facial expression is often an indication of what is going on in our heads, whether we mean for it to be that way or not.

The look we give someone can often say more to them that the words that are coming out of our mouths. We could all be a little more aware of the kinds of looks we give our kids throughout the day.

Smiling at your son is a quick and simple way to convey affection to him. A smile says "I like you. I'm glad you're here!" A smile from mom can bring sunshine into the heart of a child (or young adult). Never underestimate the power of a simple smile. Smiling can also boost our own mood and outlook as well. Next time you are frustrated or you're having a bad day, try smiling. It may be hard and it may feel fake, but it can help you feel better emotionally. Believe it or not, it's true. I used to be a doubter when it came to this particular claim—until I tried it (consistently) for myself. You know what I found out? It works!

A smile is one of the best gifts we can give to those around us. Giving your son a smile can brighten his day, improve his mood while it improves yours, and let him know you love him. Ask yourself, "Do I smile at my son regularly throughout the day?" If you do, keep on doing it! If you don't, decide you will start. Make the conscious choice to show your son your love through your facial expressions—most importantly a smile.

I'm ashamed to admit that there were many years in my career of motherhood that I did not smile at my children very often. When they looked at my face, they often saw a sullen or angry expression. I looked tired or depressed or frustrated. How do you think this made them feel? It often made them wonder if they had done something wrong to upset me. Usually, it had nothing to do with something they had done, but they didn't know that. It had simply become a habit in my life. How heartbreaking to think that my children wondered if I were angry with them simply because I had a habit of having a sour expression on my face! When I realized that I had this problem and decided to do something about it, it made such a big difference. Change in this area didn't come easy. It took me a long time to retrain myself to show a more cheerful side of myself. I had to do a lot of inner work on myself as well. The difference was well worth the effort, though. I do still have days where I don't smile as often as I should or would like to. Now, however, my children aren't left wondering if they've don't something wrong to make mommy mad at them. What a gift I am able to give to the through the simple yet profound act of smiling!

Smile at your son, dear mom. He will know by your smile that you care about him. It will bring sunshine into his world in a way few other things can. Show him on your face that you love him. Cheerfulness is a choice.

**You are loved and valued**

Showing affection to our boys in varied ways and at different intervals throughout our day can send a clear message of their importance to us. It can show them that they are valued and loved. Eye contact, a smile, a pat on the should, a hug—none of these things take that much time or effort, but they can mean the world to our sons. They can give them a sense of worth and belonging.

We love our boys, so let's show them!

# CHAPTER TEN

**Don't go it alone**

Raising sons is challenging, meaningful, and incredibly rewarding. We as moms have special challenges in raising our sons because as women, we have no idea what it's like to be male. Getting some insight into what makes males tick can be extremely valuable.

Seek input from trusted and mature men in your and your son's life. Ask your husband's advice and guidance when dealing with your son. Trust his wisdom. He knows things you will never fully understand about your sons, and that's okay. In fact, it's a good thing. He is a man, and one day your son will also be a man. Their brains are set up differently than yours. They process information in a different way than you do. Look to your husband for insight into your son's mind and actions. He will know a lot more than you will be able to learn by simple observation.

Listen to your husband when it comes to raising your son,

even if you don't necessarily agree with what he has to say. Trust that he has the inside scoop on being a boy. He was one once, remember?

If you are not in a position to utilize advice and insight from your son's father, look for another man you trust and look up to who will fill that role for you. This could be your own father or brother, or perhaps it is an older man in your church or your pastor. It could be your uncle or your neighbor. If he is a man you would like to see your sons grow up to be like in some way, he may be a good resource for information and insight into raising your son. Ask him for his advice on a particular situation, or just in general. Most men, if they are good and worthy of being asked for advice, will willingly give you help and guidance if needed.

Men have a perspective on boyhood I (and you) as a woman cannot fully understand because I have never been a boy. How can I hope to fully understand and identify with what it is like to be a boy when I have not, nor will I ever be, a boy? Because of this fact, I value greatly the perspective that the men in my life can offer as I raise my own five sons. My husband has so much wisdom to add to my understanding as a mother because he is willing to let me know at times that my boys are just being boys.

There have been many times over the years when I have watched my sons doing something I can't begin to understand the reasoning behind. I have then turned to my husband and asked him "why?" and he has responded by stating, matter-of-factly, that "that's just what boys do."

Oh, okay.

For instance, there was the time when I discovered that two of my sons were playing with matches. Obviously, I was extremely upset (read FREAKED OUT) by this discovery. I immediately jumped to the conclusion that my sons were juvenile delinquents destined for a life of crime. What were we going to do about this?! My husband, who is usually the one who freaks out first, remained eerily calm in this particular instance. He had an "I am not surprised by this in the least" look on his face. Apparently, as my husband explained, this particular activity is a rite of passage for many teenage boys.

To ease my mind even further, he proceeded to tell me the story of when, as a teenage boy himself, he and a friend made rocket fuel and then lit it on fire—in his bedroom. At least our sons were playing with fire outside. Of course, both my husband and I sternly warned the boys about the dangers associated with their recent experiment. We emphasized the importance of safety and prudence. We lectured them on the foolishness of their decision. We took disciplinary measures in the form of revoked privileges, just to be sure they knew we were serious. It's just that my husband didn't seem surprised that our sons had decided to act in this manner. It didn't shock and disturb him in the same way it did me.

And that baffled me.

For as long as I have known my husband (and even before that), he has been telling stories of all the crazy things he did as a kid. For instance, there was the time he chopped the tree down on his younger brother and, when he left to find someone to help get the tree off, he subsequently forgot about his brother lying under the tree—for about 20 minutes. Granted, it was a small tree and his brother was eventually rescued and came out completely unharmed. Then there was the time he jumped from the hayloft and into a hay pile, only to discover that he had landed just inches from a pitchfork protruding from the hay. These stories were just a few of many he has shared with me over the years.

So it shouldn't have surprised me that our sons' poor choice of entertainment didn't surprised my husband. He did even worse and more dangerous things when he was a boy, and lived to tell the tales.

My father told me stories over the years of things he did as a boy that would make most mothers cringe. Being the calm, mild-mannered gentleman that my father was, it was always a little hard for me to reconcile the stories he told of his boyhood with the man he had grown up to become. In his boyhood, he did things like build a fire in the bottom of his father's fishing boat and force-feed the chickens on their farm until many of them died. He also had a surprising destructive streak as a youngster, demonstrated by the choice he and his older brother made to throw rocks at the windows in the barn, eventually managing to break every single pane of glass in the entire building. He survived all his own shenanigans as well and lived to tell his tales of boyhood to his great-grandchildren.

It is situations like these that put my motherly protectiveness into perspective. I need my husband's insight and experience to balance my own perspective. When I was a girl, I would never have dreamed of doing most of the things my sons try. Boys can be reckless. My husband was even more reckless and heedless than my sons have even thought of being. This gives me some small comfort.

There are other areas where my husband's experience as a man can help me understand boys. Take puberty, for instance. I have absolutely no idea what it is like to think like an adolescent boy. If I knew what they were actually thinking, I would probably be terrified. But my husband knows, and it does not terrify him. He lived through it himself. The wisdom he has gained as he has grown and matured can be a great asset in giving our sons advice and guidance.

Value your husbands input in bringing up your son. Don't take it for granted. And if you don't have the involvement of a husband in raising your son, be sure to seek out that wise older man who will act as a mentor for your son. As he grows and matures, he will need the input of a man in his life.

Boys also need the camaraderie that relationships with other men bring. Hanging out with mom isn't quite the same as spending time with the guys. It has its place of importance, of course, but most moms probably aren't interested in the kinds of activities that a boy would do with another male. I know I personally would not be able to teach my sons how to bait a hook, or skin a muskrat, or build a treehouse. My husband can teach them all those things, and much more. (Actually, my husband has taught our daughters some of these things, too!) Even in this age of "Girl Power" it just takes a man to do certain things well.

Boys need men in their lives. They need to spend time with men, doing manly things, without the interference of a mother. We don't know how to be male; the only people who can teach our sons how to be male are other men. Trust that your son needs men in his life to be role models of manhood.

# CHAPTER ELEVEN

Throughout this book, we have discussed the challenges and joys of moms raising boys. It's not always easy to bring up a son. As a mom, you've faced days when you want to scream in frustration. You've also faced days when the sticky kisses and pudgy arms around your neck bring you more joy than you thought was possible to experience. Motherhood is like that. Being a mom of boys can be a rollercoaster ride sometimes. It can swing between exhausting and exhilarating. It can open up a whole world you never knew existed before your little boy came into your life. And it is always, without question, an exciting adventure.

In these final thoughts, we come to what I deem the most important aspect of a mom raising a son—celebrating boyhood. We have an obligation as moms of boys to embrace to beautiful, messy, noisy adventure of raising these future men. What a privilege and a joy! Don't take even one moment of this journey for granted. You are raising a future world changer. Believe it, embrace it, act like it!

Let us celebrate the amazing and unique qualities boys bring to the table. Putting value on the traits and gifts boys offer the world will help develop those gifts to be even more meaningful and valuable to both our boys and those around them.

There are 5 key areas where boys bring special gifts to the world that should be celebrated as the treasures they are.

## 1. Potential

Your son is quite possibly destined to change the world. At the very least, he is meant to make an impact in the arena in which he will someday operate. He may be a husband and father someday. Or he may be a church leader. Maybe he'll lead a company or business. Or perhaps he'll be a speaker or influencer of some kind. Your job is to get him ready of whatever role God calls him to. Help him to believe in himself by believing in him yourself. Celebrate his amazing potential.

When you look at your son, do you see only the boy he is or can you see the man he will someday become? Develop a vision for what he could be and speak that into his life with your words and actions. Have faith that God will fulfill His purpose in your son's heart and life and teach your son to have that same faith. Show him how to see his own potential and give him a vision for what he can become.

Each of our sons is a powerhouse of limitless potential. When placed in the hands of a great God, they can do great things for His glory. Never doubt what God can do in and through your son's life.

## 2. Perspective

Boys offer a unique perspective on the world completely unlike girls. They see things differently. Remember, research shows that the male and female brain are very different from one another in how they function. Your son views the world from a different viewpoint—and that's great!

Celebrate the unique and wonderful perspective boys bring to the world. Their sense of wonder and adventure offer excitement and an enthusiasm that can be contagious.

Imagine how boring it would be if everyone thought the same way about everything. There would be no variety in personalities. What a wonderful thing our differences can be!

Take the time and effort to see things from your son's point of view sometimes. I guarantee it differs from yours and that you will learn something from him as a result of this effort. View the world through his eyes and you will discover things you never knew were there before. Let a whole new view on the world open up before you as you place yourself in your son's perspective. It will change your own perspective.

## 3. Enthusiasm

Boys have a natural enthusiasm for life that is infectious. They jump into new situations with both feet and embrace what is in front them with gusto. I know that I as a cautious, sometimes overly protective mom can learn a lot from all of my sons about living in the moment. I watch my boys enjoying life and the opportunities in their path and I want to be more like that myself.

Enthusiasm can be funneled into focus and productivity given the right conditions. Foster your son's enthusiasm, wherever it may be directed. Celebrate and encourage your son to wholeheartedly pour himself into the things he loves.

## 4. Leadership

Our sons are designed to be leaders. Someday, all of our boys will be leaders in one capacity or other. They will be fathers, husbands, church leaders, business owners, department heads, teachers. Perhaps they won't fill a formal leadership role, but they will have someone or something following them at some point in their lives. Help them prepare for that by fostering the natural leadership qualities in them. In this age of feminism, boys are often relegated to the back seat when it comes to encouraging leadership. Don't let that happen to your son. Celebrate the abilities for leadership he displays and encourage him to develop them to their fullest extent. He'll be better prepared for whatever God has called him to do with his life.

Leadership is a gift and a responsibility. Our sons need to know that they can and should be good, godly leaders to the ones God will put under their authority. They need to develop in themselves the traits of kindness, compassion, flexibility, self-discipline, decisiveness, and a willingness to blaze a trail for others. Find and nature those traits in your son. Celebrate him as a leader-in-training!

## 5. Vision

Lastly, celebrate your son's vision for the future. Develop a vision for his future for yourself. Encourage him to dream big and go for those dreams. Teach him to never let fear or uncertainty stand in the way of him achieving his dreams. As the Bible says, "Where there is no vision, the people perish." Celebrate your son as he creates a vision for his life. That's how he will change the world for Christ!

Let's celebrate boys!

Boys are fascinating and amazing creatures. Yes, at times they baffle us moms. At other times, though, they make us beam with love and pride. There is nothing quite like being the mother of a son. The bond that develops is strong. With a lot of effort and a ton of grace, we can raise good, godly, amazing sons, even in this world which often seems hostile to anything connected with being male. I guarantee, if you raise your son well, when he is grown, he will be forever grateful to you for the sacrifices and love you poured into him. Often, good men who were raised by good and loving mothers proudly proclaim that they owe much of who they have become to their mothers.

Wouldn't you love to have your son "rise up and call you

blessed" someday? Sure, some days are really hard. There will be days when you are exhausted from chasing your toddler boy around—believe me, I've been there. (I'm still there on many days.) There will be days when you wish you had several sets of arms so you can keep up with all the demands of motherhood. You will have time when you shake your head in confusion as to why your son did something. There will be rock collections in the dryer vent and matchbox cars stuck in the sink drain. You will find random sticks lying around the house for no explainable reason. There will be days when you will worry about your son's safety as he makes yet another risky choice.

Take heart, dear mom, because you will survive. It will be worth every noisy, dirty, sticky, scary moment of mothering this son of yours. You are helping to create a man. That's not an easy feat, but it is an immeasurably worthy one. Do it well, and do not grow weary. Cherish every moment, every stage—none of them ever last.

Embrace the messy, crazy life of the mom of a boy. There's nothing like it.

# NOTES

Chapter 1

1. *Studies Show Significant Differences in Brains of Men and Women,* Michael Price https://stanmed.stanford.edu/2017spring/how-mens-and-womens-brains-are-different.html

*Brain Differences Between Genders,* Gregory L. Jantz, PhD https://www.psychologytoday.com/blog/hope-relationships/201402/brain-differences-between-genders

Chapter 2

2. *The Real Difference Between Boys and Girls,* Anita Sethi, PhD http://www.parenting.com/article/real-difference-between-boys-and-girls

3. *Boys' And Girls' Brains Are Different: Gender Differences In Language Appear Biological,* Northwestern University.

ScienceDaily. ScienceDaily, 5 March 2008 www.science-daily.com/releases/2008/03/080303120346.htm

4.   *Raising Boys and Girls: Differences in Development*, Baby Center Medical Advisory Board, BabyCenter.com https://www.babycenter.com/0_raising-boys-and-girls-differ-ences-in-development_3659011.bc

5.   *Why Do Boys Engage in More Risk Taking Than Girls? The Role of Attributions, Beliefs, and Risk Appraisals*, Barbara A. Morrongiello, PhD. Journal of Pediatric Psychology, Vol. 23, No. 1, 1998, pp. 33—43 https://academic.oup.com/jpepsy/article-pdf/23/1/33/2702257/23-1-33.pdf

6.   *Are Girls Easier to Potty Train Than Boys?* PottyTrain-ingConcepts.com   http://www.pottytrainingconcepts.com/A-Girls-Easier-Potty-Train.html

7.   *Male Aggression: Why Are Men More Violent?*, Dorian Fortuna, PhD   https://www.psychologytoday.com/blog/homo-aggressivus/201409/male-aggression

Chapter 4

8.   *Male Aggression: Why Are Men More Violent?*, Dorian Fortuna, PhD   https://www.psychologytoday.com/blog/homo-aggressivus/201409/male-aggression

Chapter 5

9.   *Average American Watches 5 Hours of TV Per Day*, Report Shows, David Hinckley   http://www.nyda-

ilynews.com/life-style/average-american-watch-es-5-hours-tv-day-article-1.1711954

10. *What Screen Time Can Really Do to Kids Brains*, Liraz Margalit, PhD  https://www.psychologytoday.com/blog/behind-online-behavior/201604/what-screen-time-can-really-do-kids-brains

11. The Effects of Violent Video Games: Do they affect our behavior?, Brad J. Bushman, Ph.D  http://ithp.org/articles/violentvideogames.html

12. *Parenting in the Age of Online Pornography*, Nick Bilton  https://www.nytimes.com/2015/01/08/style/parenting-in-the-age-of-online-porn.html

Chapter 6

13. The Holy Bible, English Standard Version. ESV® Text Edition: 2016. Copyright © 2001 by Crossway Bibles, a publishing ministry of Good News Publishers.

Chapter 7

14. *U.S. Department of Education: Homeschooling Continues to Grow!*, J. Michael Smith, Esq.  https://www.hslda.org/docs/news/2013/201309030.asp

15. *Research Facts on Homeschooling*, Brian D. Ray, Ph.D.  https://www.nheri.org/research/research-facts-on-homeschooling.html

Chapter 8

16.    *Mother and Son: The Respect Effect*, Emerson Egger-ichs, PhD, Thomas Nelson Publishers, April 5, 2016

Chapter 9

17.    *Loving Touch Is Key to Healthy Brain Development*, Christopher Bergland    https://www.psychologytoday.com/blog/the-athletes-way/201310/loving-touch-is-key-healthy-brain-development

18.    *The Health Benefits of Hugging*, Stacey Colino https://health.usnews.com/health-news/health-wellness/articles/2016-02-03/the-health-benefits-of-hugging

19.    *How Much of Communication is Really Nonverbal?*, Blake    http://www.nonverbalgroup.com/2011/08/how-much-of-communication-is-really-nonverbal

# RECOMMENDED RESOURCES

*Love and Respect* by Emmerson Eggerich

*The Excellent Wife* by Martha Peace

*Bringing Up Boys* by Dr. James Dobson

*Future Men* by Douglas Wilson

*Raising Real Men* by Hal and Melanie Young

*Boyhood and Beyond* by Bob Schultz

*Mother and Son: The Respect Effect* by Emmerson Eggerich

# ABOUT THE AUTHOR

Kimberly Miller began dreaming of becoming an author at the age of eight years old. Books and reading have always been her passion, and writing has given her a way to unite that love of books with history, another passion of hers. The victorian era in particular holds a special fascination for her, perhaps from reading so many L.M. Montgomery books as a child. She often feels that she was born a century too late.

Kimberly's days are kept busy homeschooling and caring for her large and often chaotic household of eight children. She and her husband live with their brood on 19 acres in rural Maine. There they keep horses, chickens, ducks, dogs, parakeets, and a snail.

To learn more about Kimberly and her books, visit her website at kimberlycmiller.com.

# ALSO BY THE AUTHOR

Escape to the beautiful island of Martha's Vineyard in the 1800s with the Cottage City Chronicles Christian inspirational romance series.

Book 1: *Adelaide's Song*

He is the proud son of a wealthy industrialist. She is the devout daughter of a respected minister. When their paths cross and sparks fly, will they be able to find common ground? William Hanson is not a happy man. Forced to spend the summer at a religious retreat, he is anything but pleased with the direction his life has taken. He is a man of strong ideals, but expressing his views has gotten him into trouble one time too many. Adelaide Holbrook is content with her simple life. She has been looking forward to spending the summer at Cottage City on the beautiful island of Martha's Vineyard. The village of pristine little seaside cottages and sparkling blue waters is the perfect setting for something special to happen. Still, when she meets William, she is not expecting the strong emotions he evokes in her. He's a man at a crossroads, forced to make a choice. She's a woman newly awakened to the possibilities of love. Will the two find a way to bridge the gap between them?

Book 2: *Hannah's Journey*

Friends from childhood, Hannah and James drifted apart after James made a rash decision that changed the course of both their lives. Now, they've been given a second chance, but illness and ambition may drive them apart. Hannah is fighting a life threatening illness. At last, it seems she may be able to overcome it. But circumstances conspire to make that impossible. James is an aspiring missionary. But hostile relations have made his mission more challenging and much more dangerous. When his life hangs in the balance, Hannah must make a crucial choice. Can Hannah face her fears and find the strength to fight for the man she loves? Will their love be strong enough to conquer sickness, separation, and even death?

Book 3: *Elliot's Choice* (Coming Spring 2019)

The two Hanson brothers come from wealth and privilege. Although they have so many advantages in life, neither one is content with the path that has been laid out before him. Both of them are searching for something just beyond their reach. When a beautiful and exotic young heiress enters their world, a fierce competition erupts between the two brothers. Jealousy sparks a conflict that neither of them is prepared for. Which brother will win the hand of the lady? And will the loser find the grace to move on and find hope and comfort for his wounded heart?

*Daughters of the Past: A Historical Fiction Anthology*

Taste the past with a collection of novellas from five decorated authors spanning ancient times to the last century. Experience love, tragedy, faith, and acceptance with these five women and their courageous journeys!

Printed in Great Britain
by Amazon

29217533R00064